Copyright © 2016 Crude Carol

Swear Word Coloring Book

All Rights Reserved Worldwide

SWEAR WORD
COLORING BOOK
LEWD STRESS RELIEF

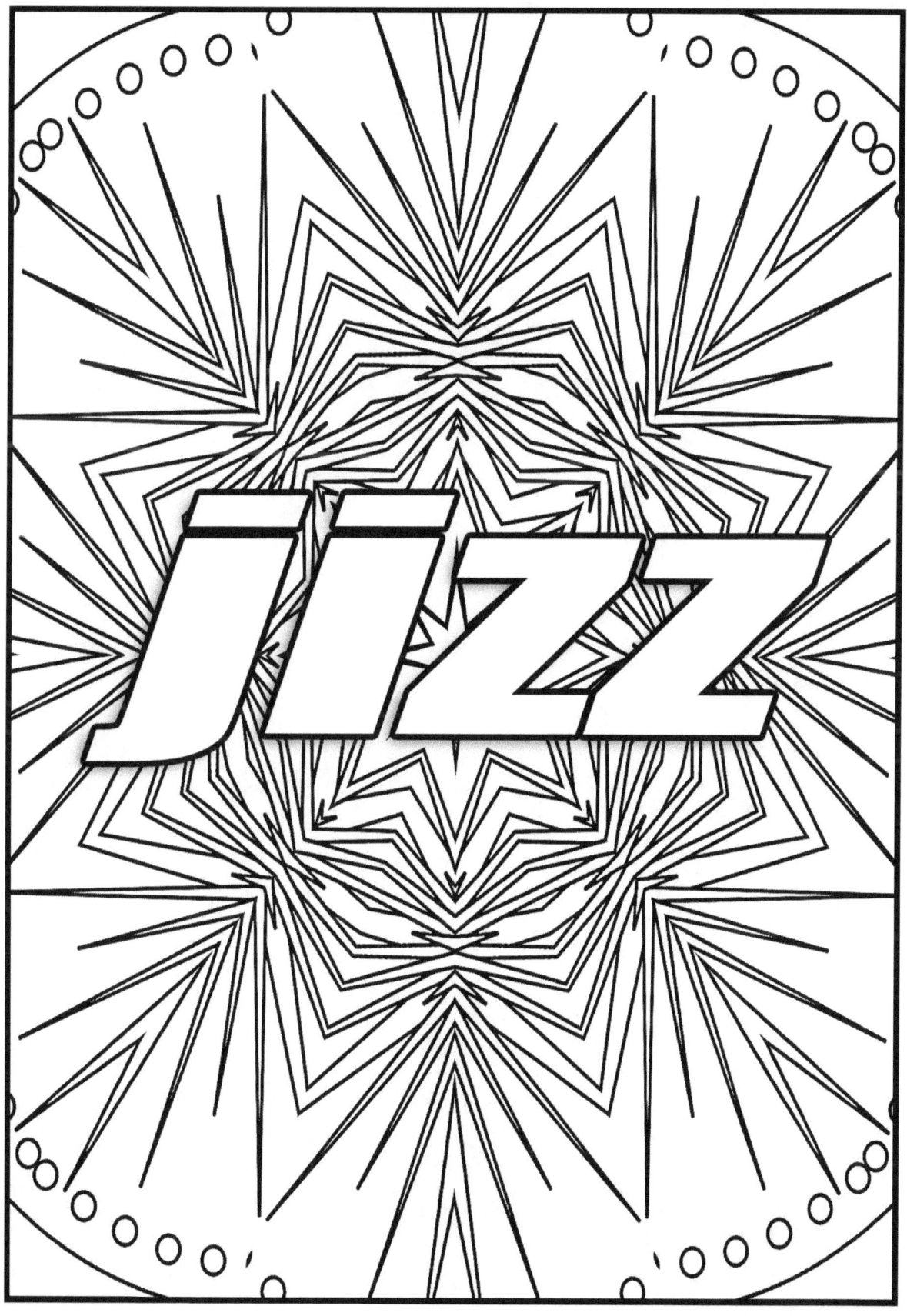

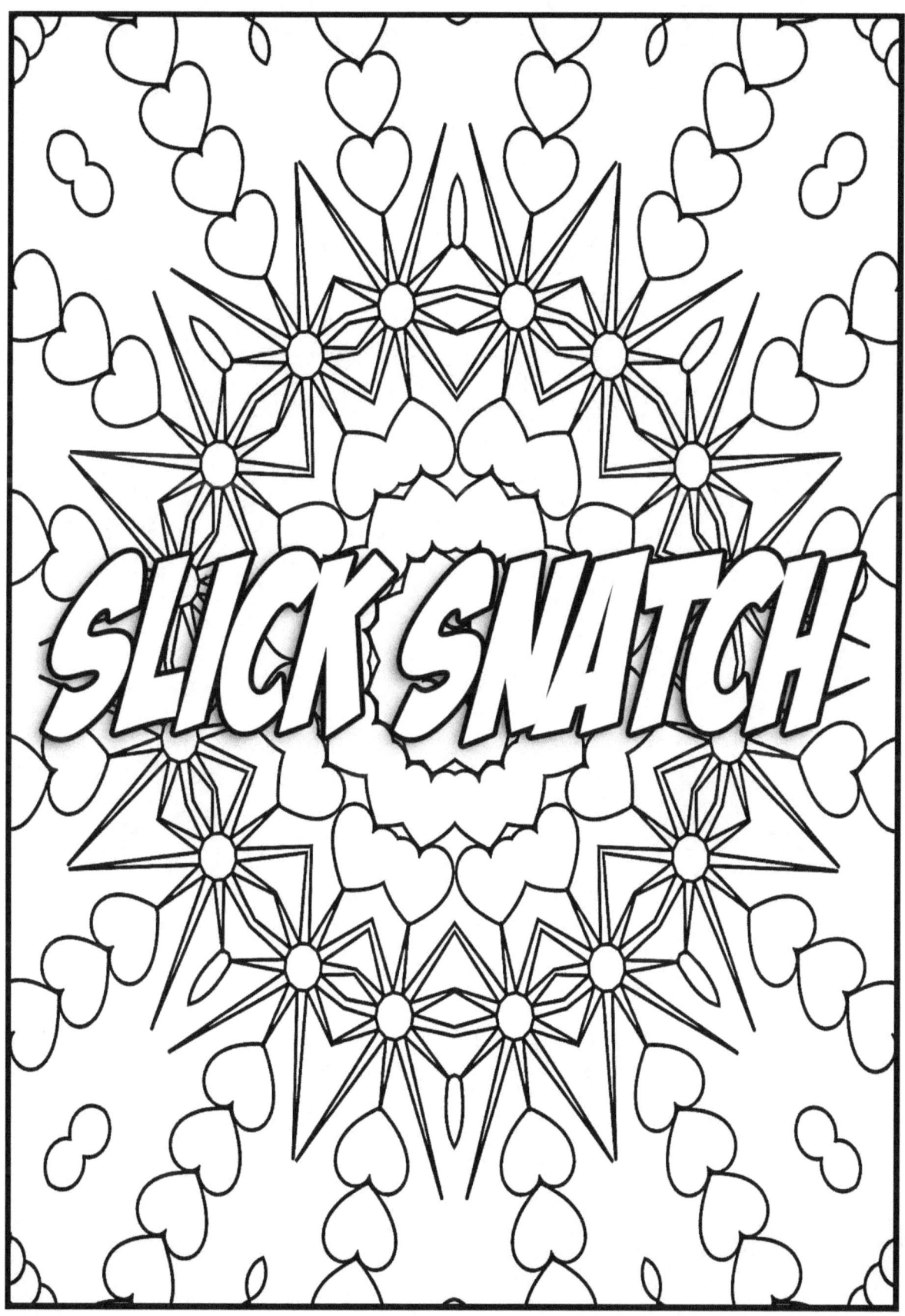

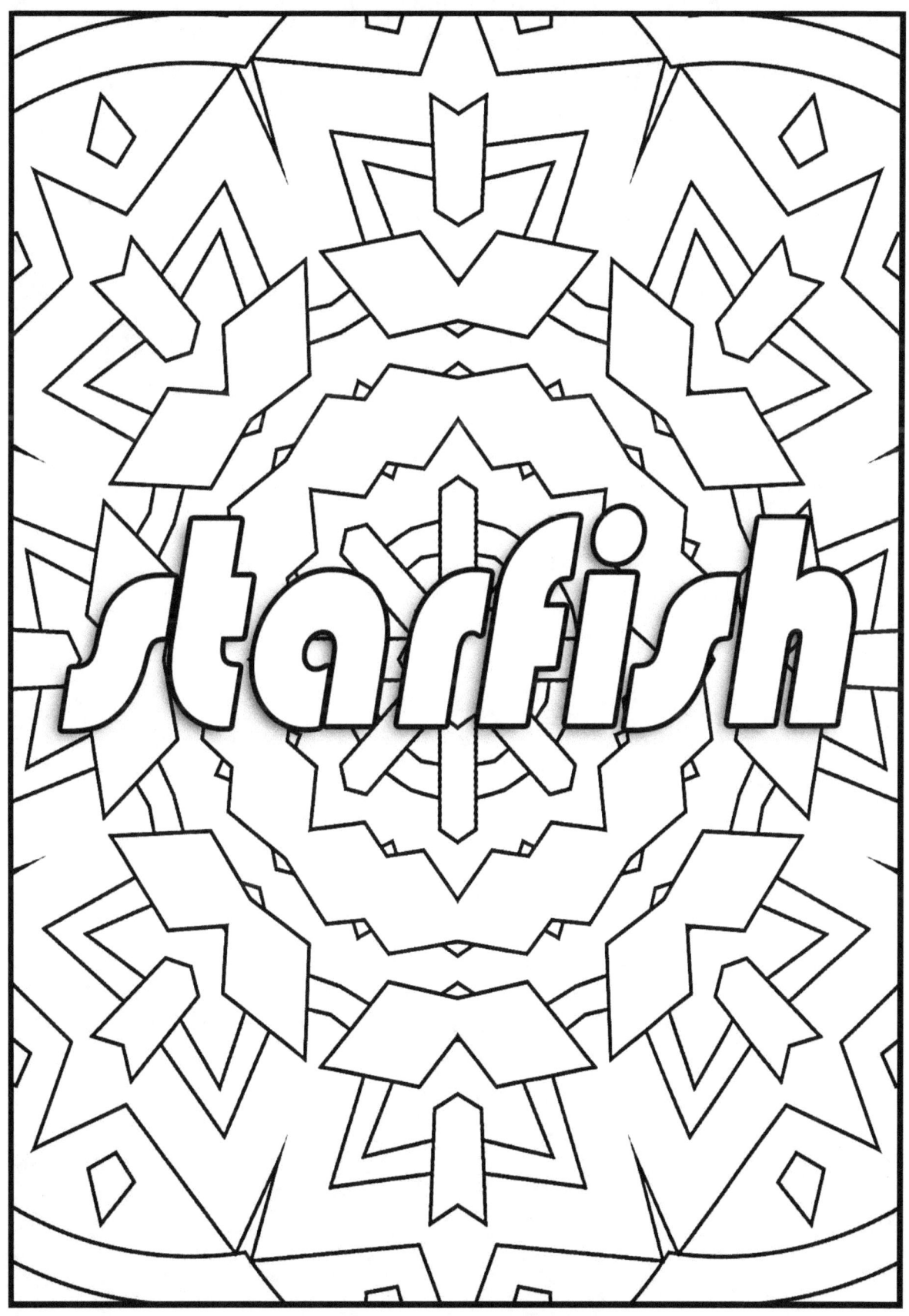

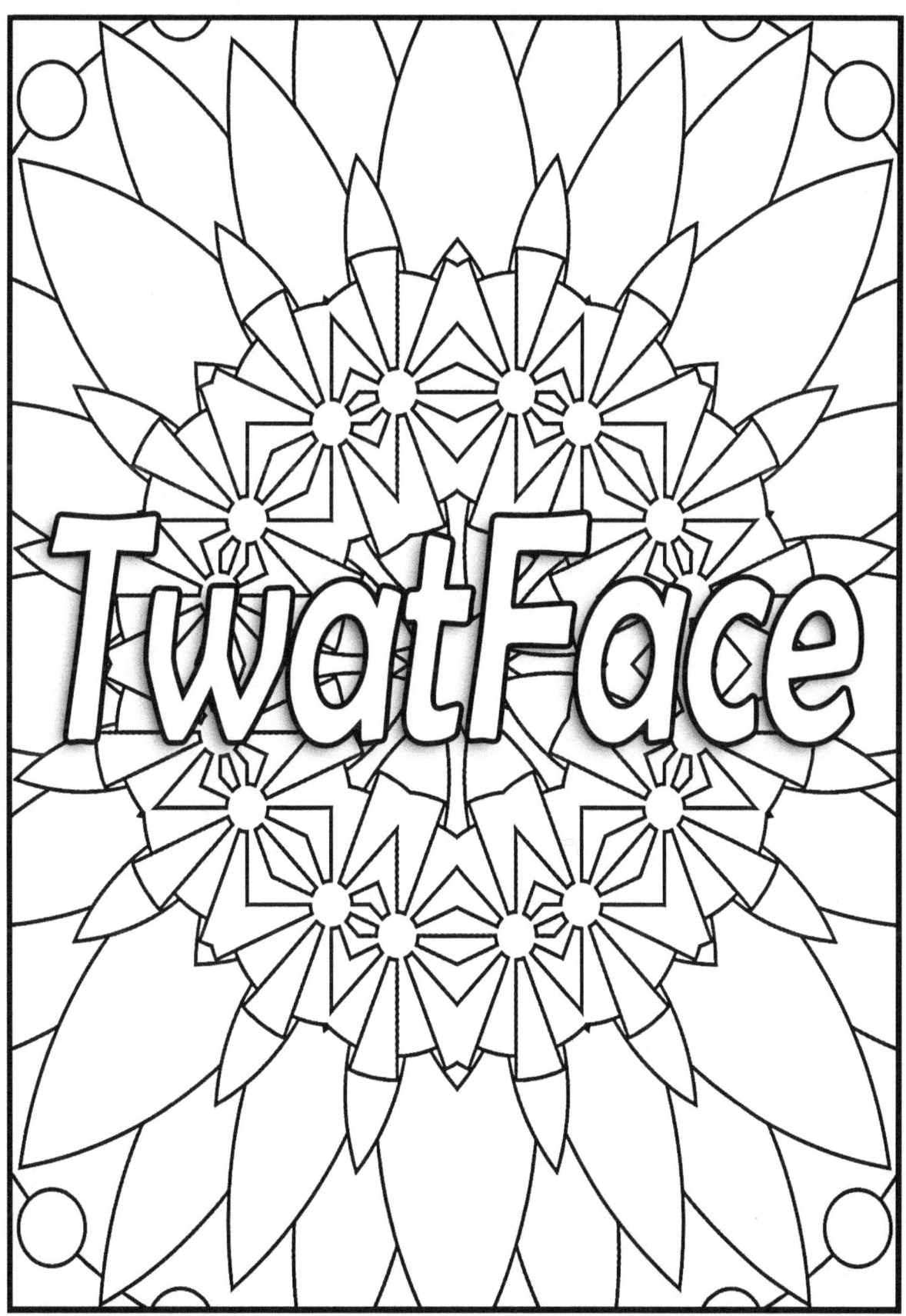

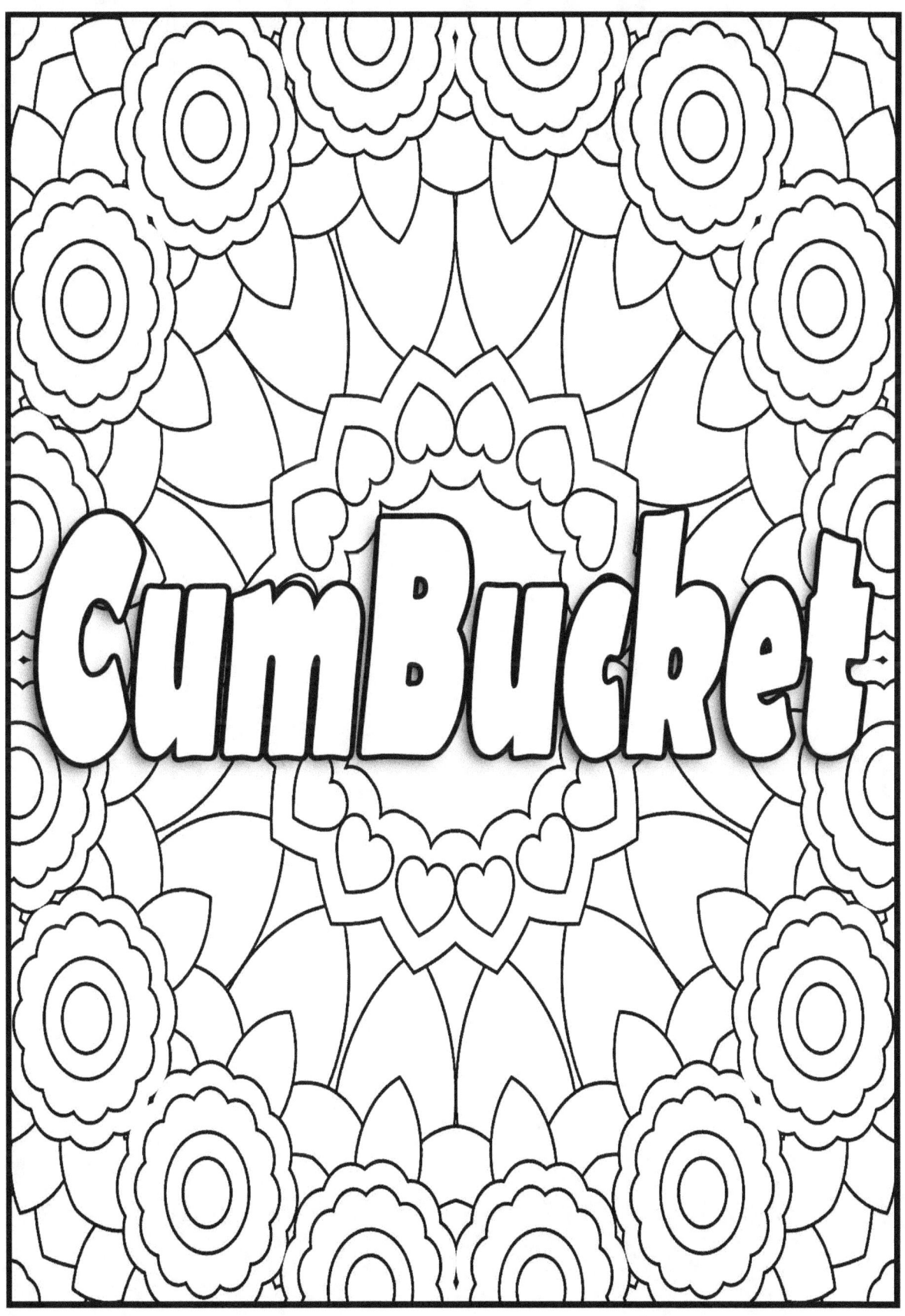

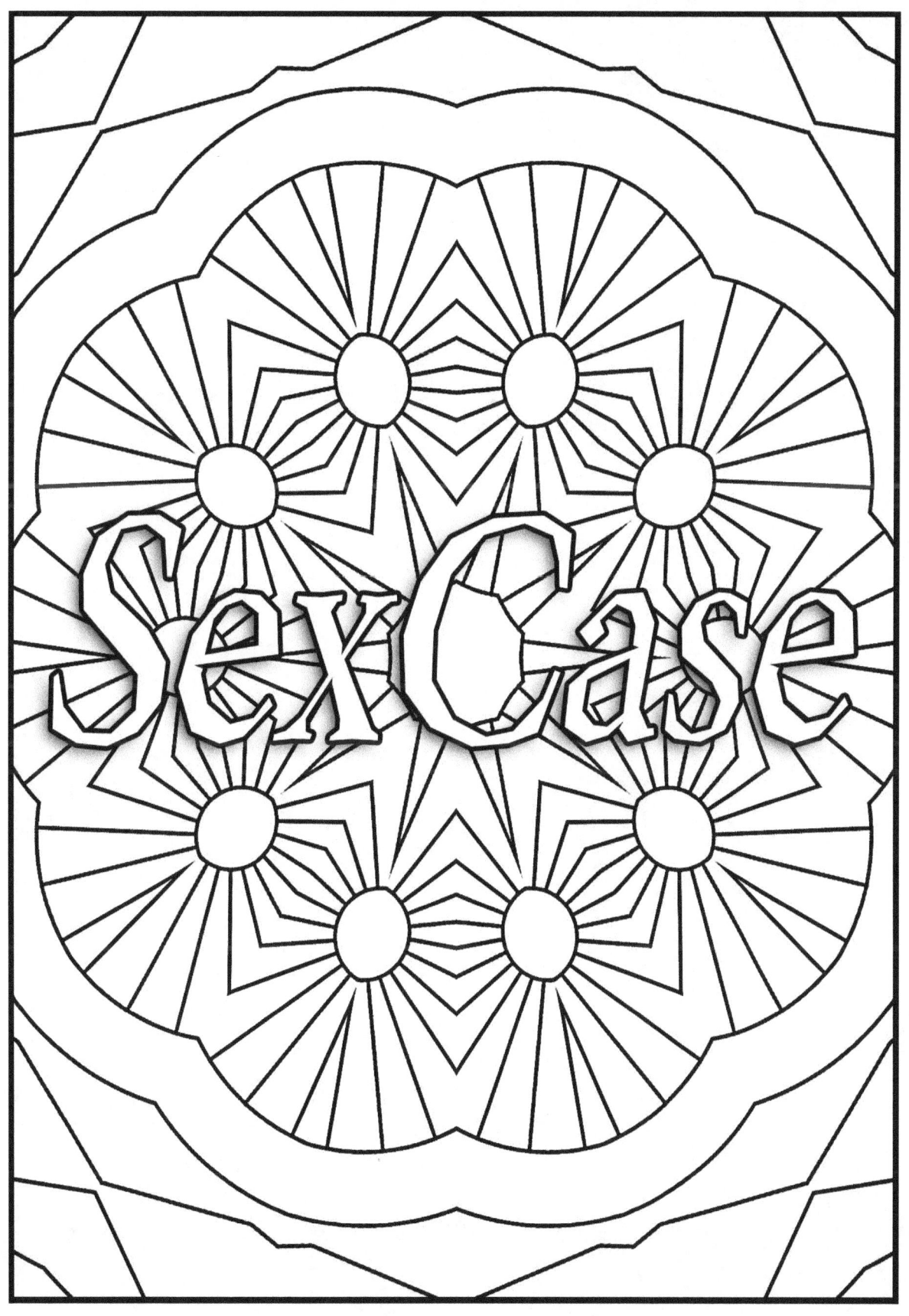

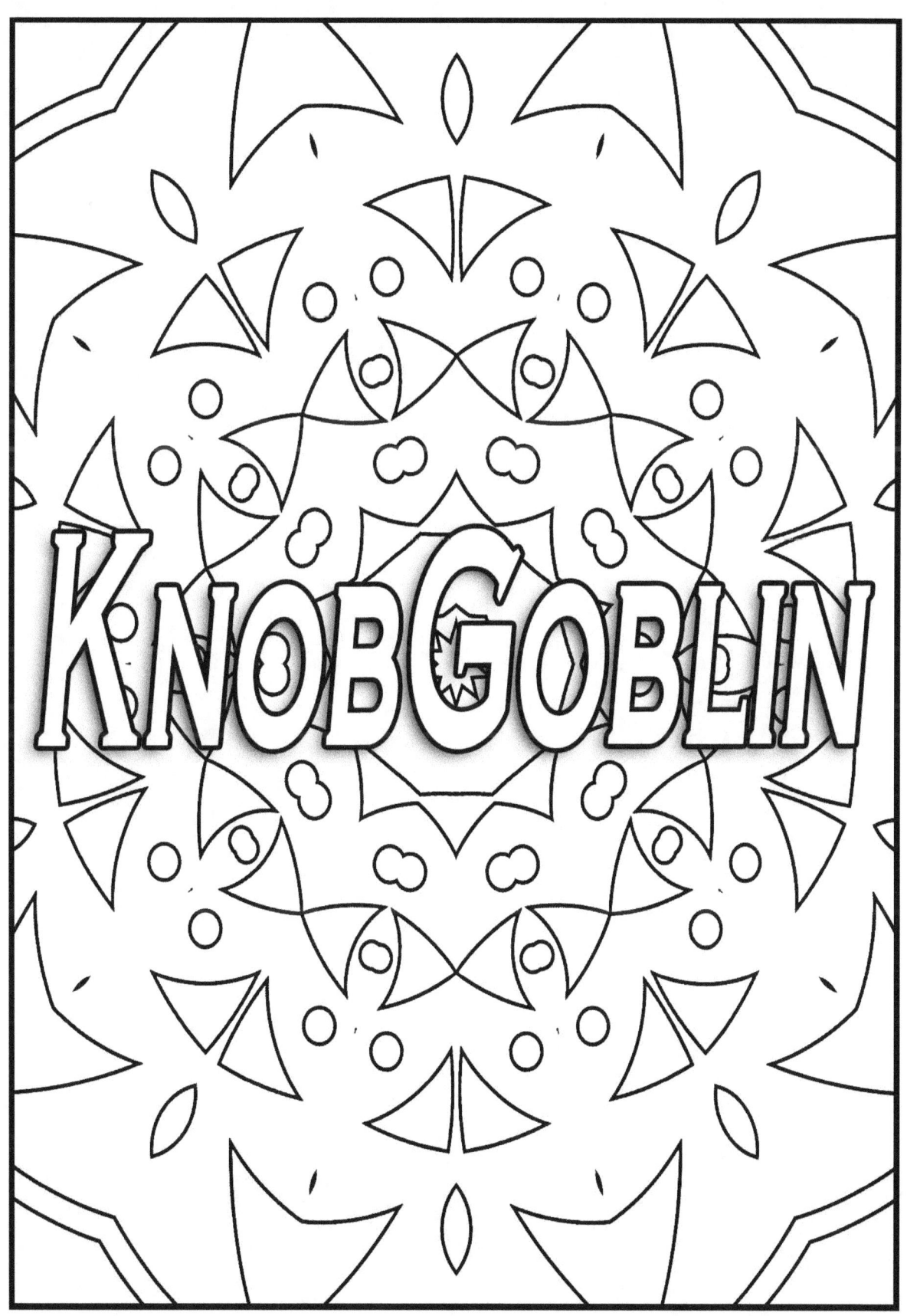

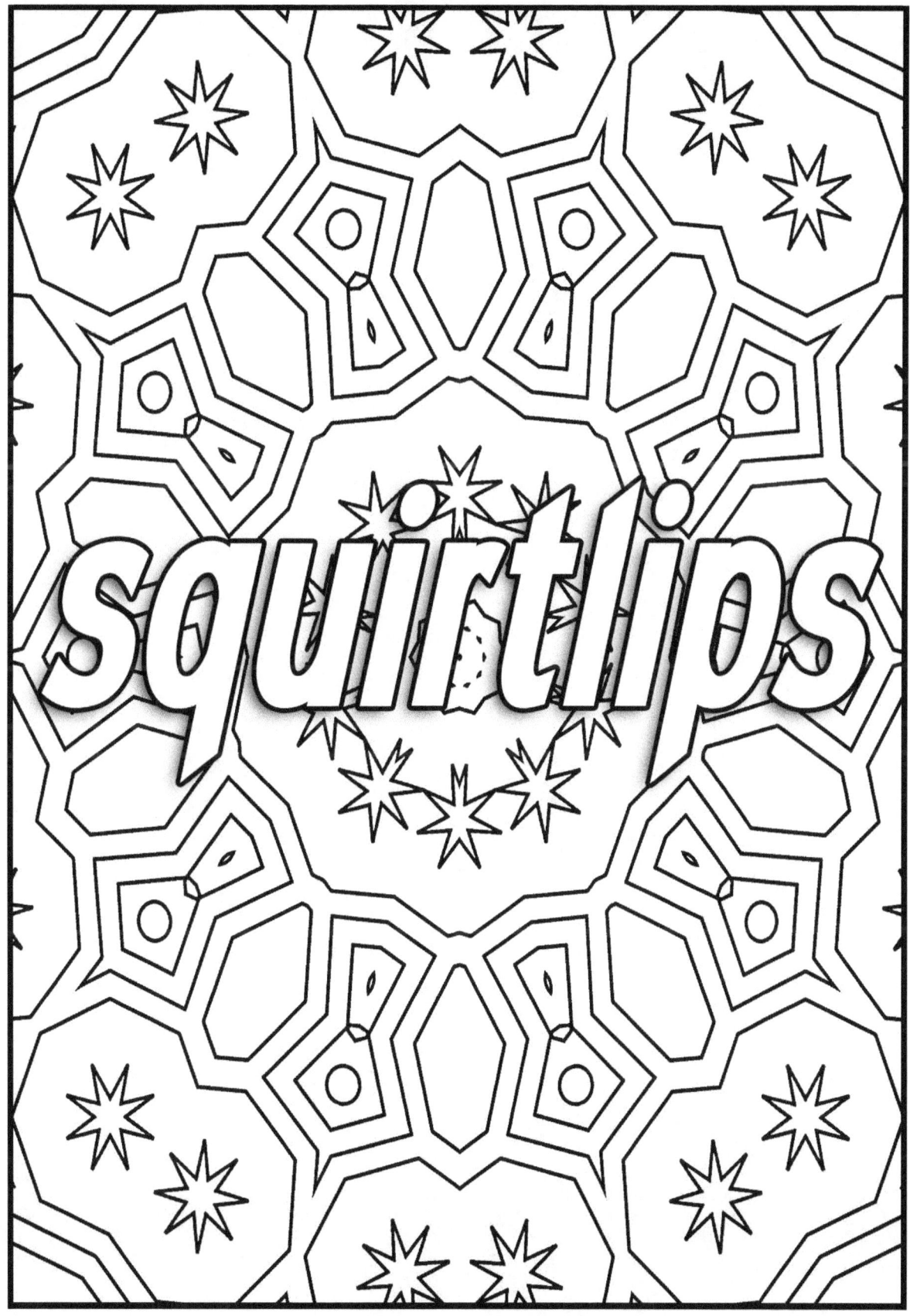

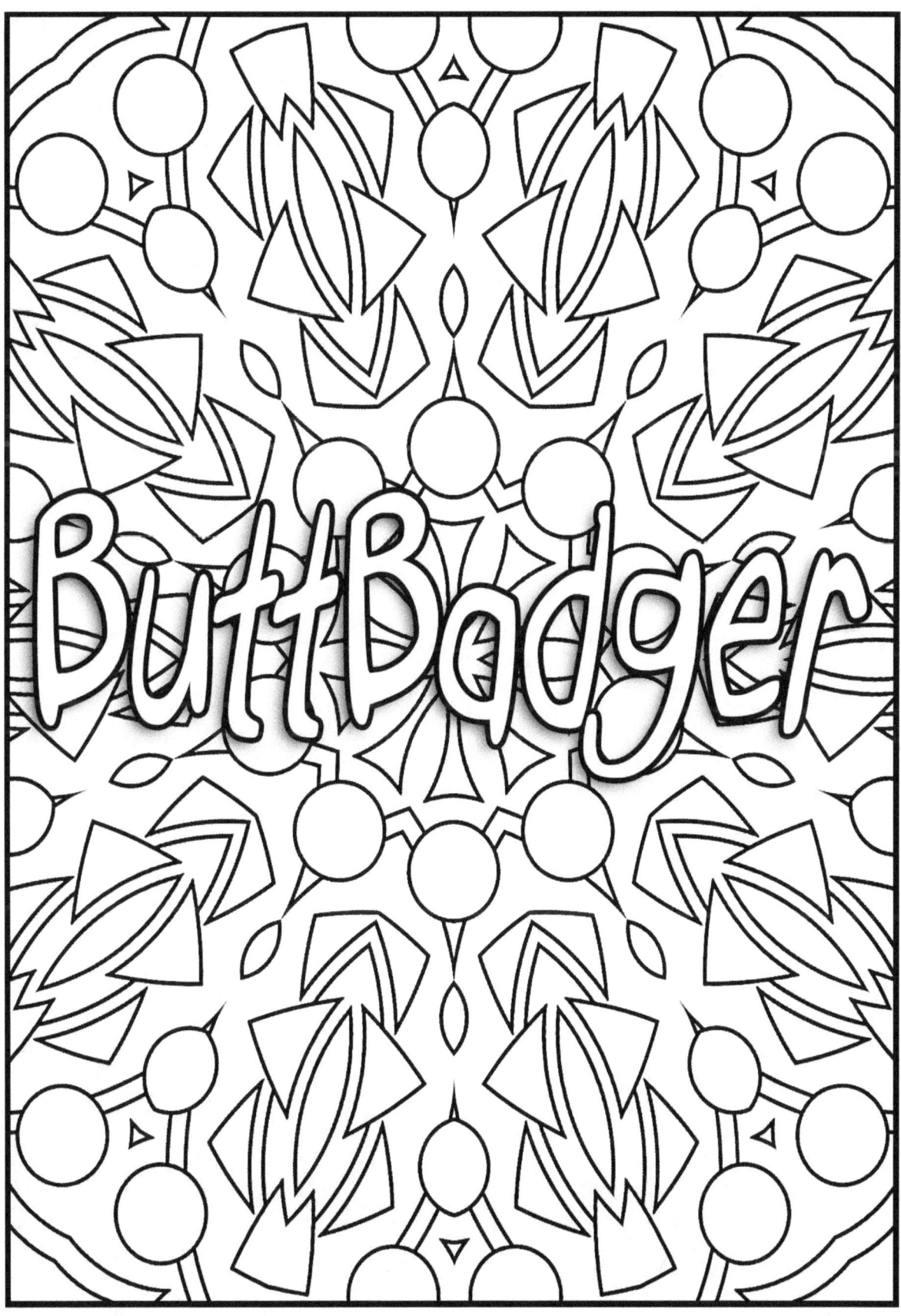

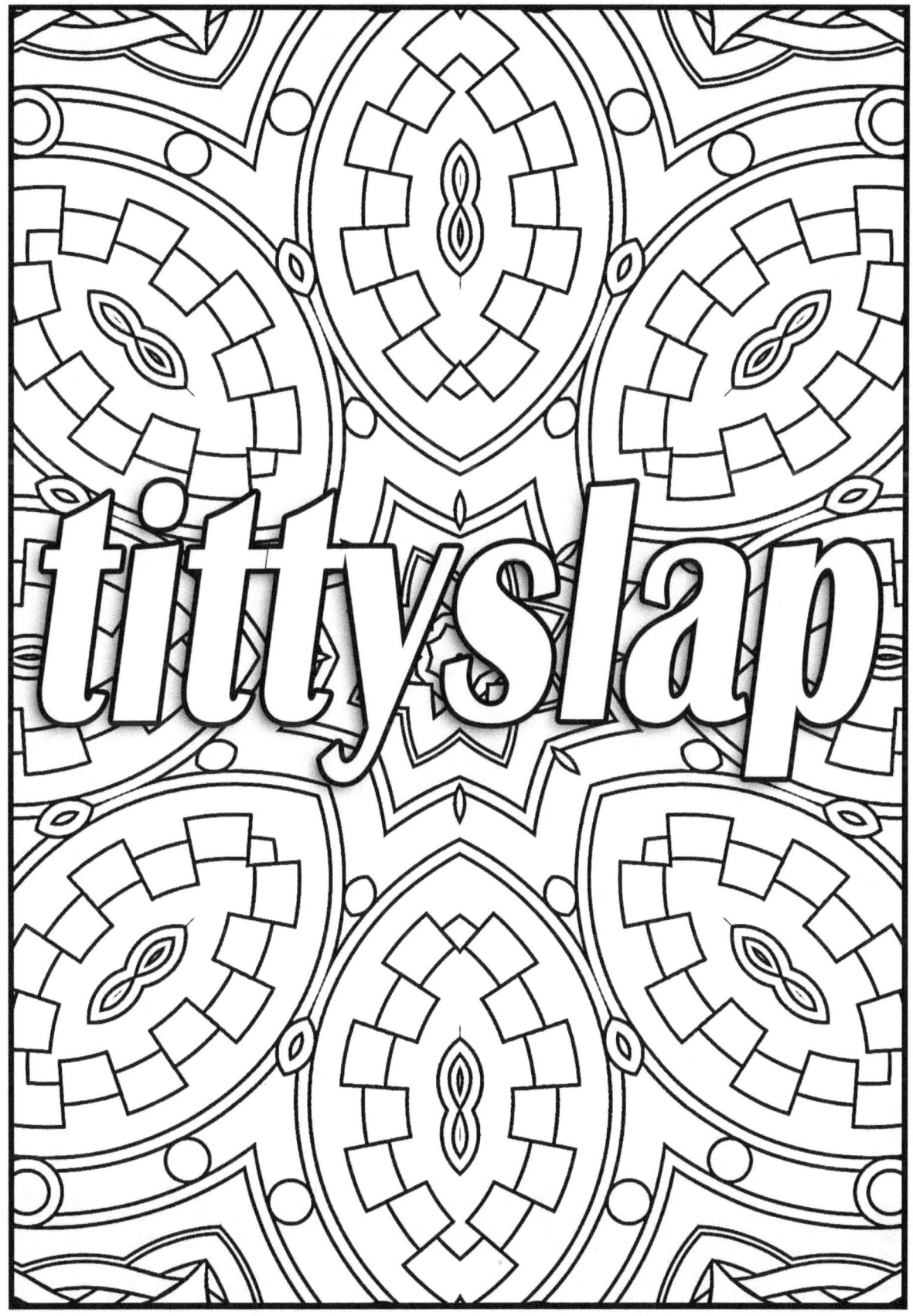

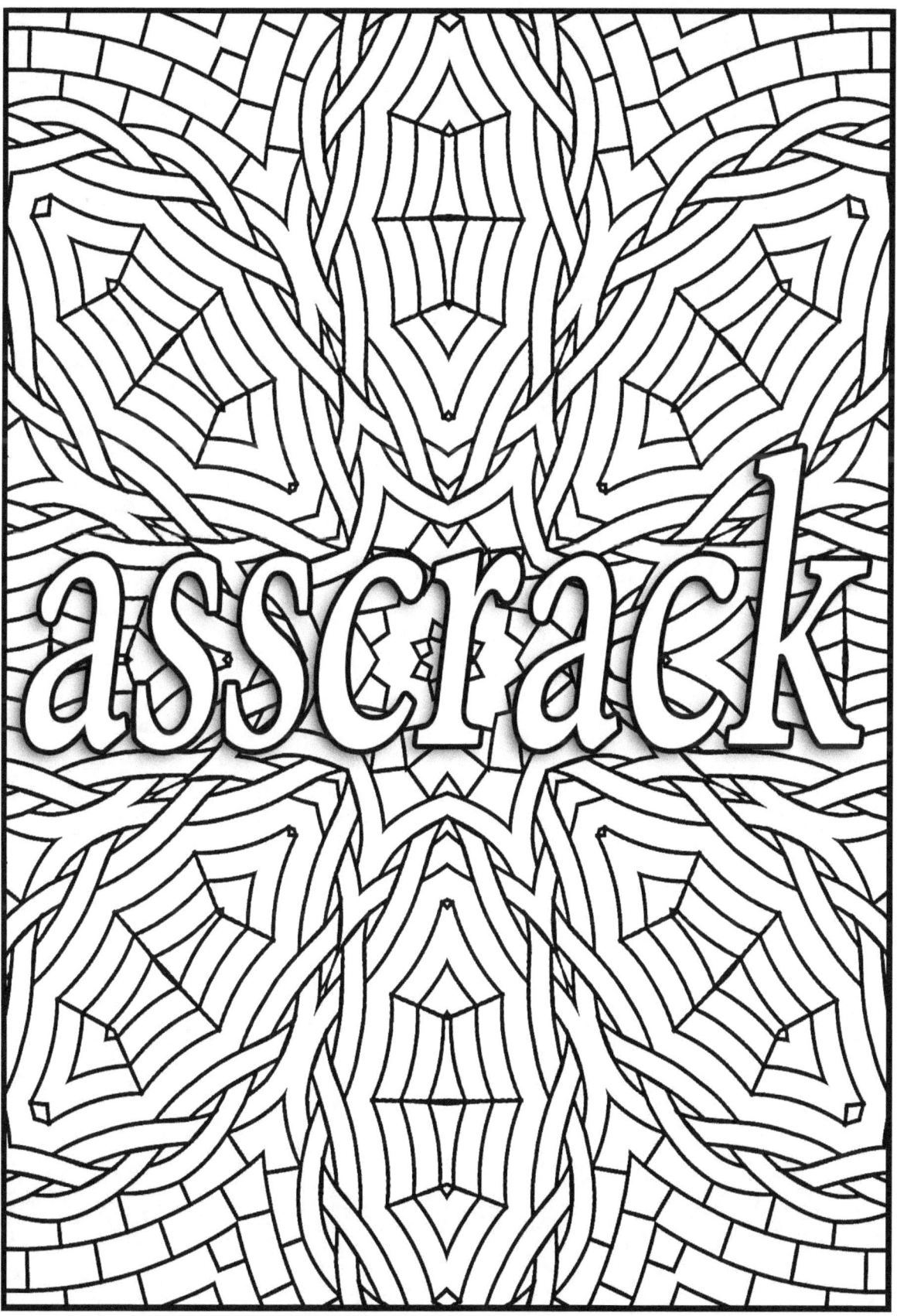

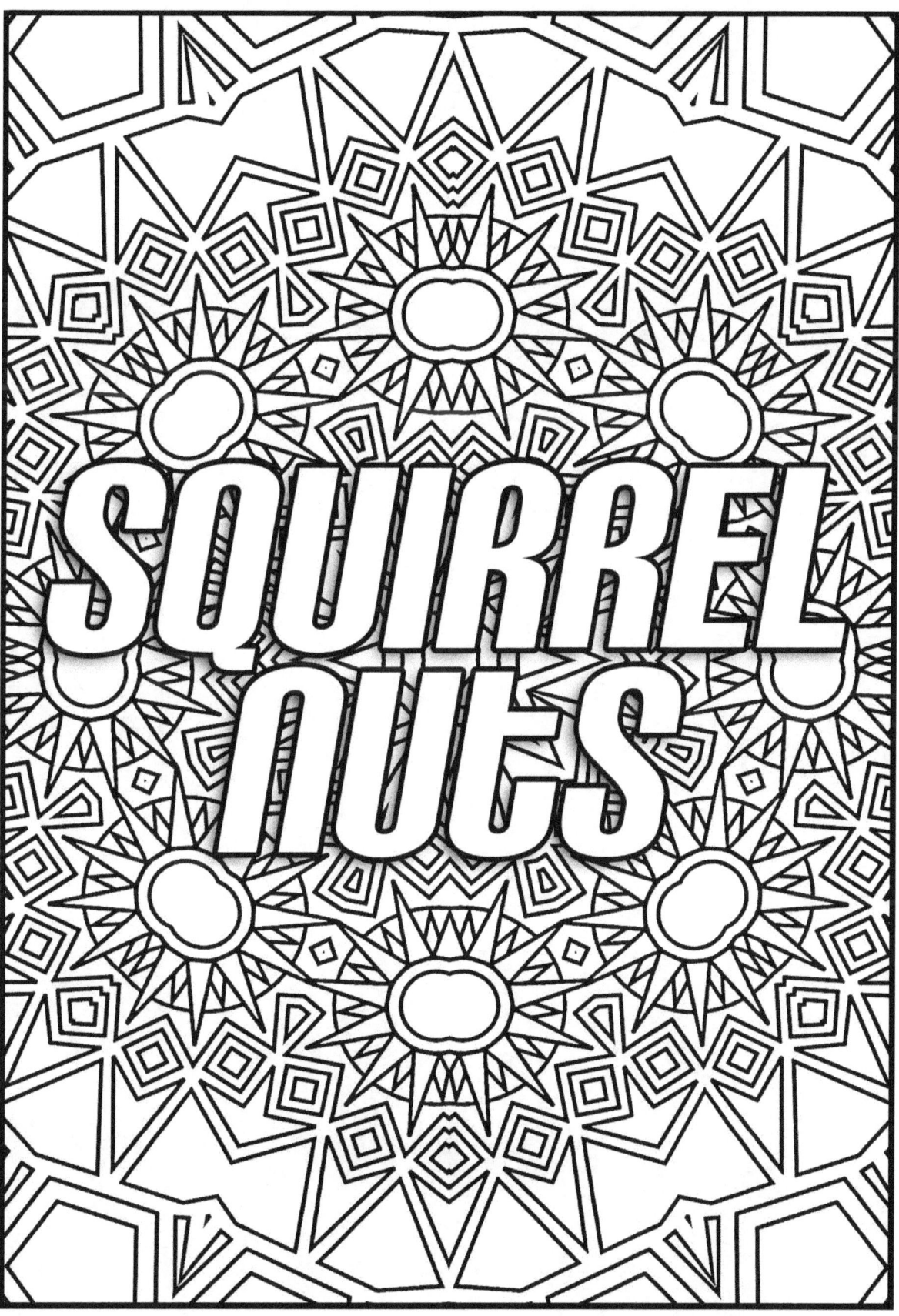

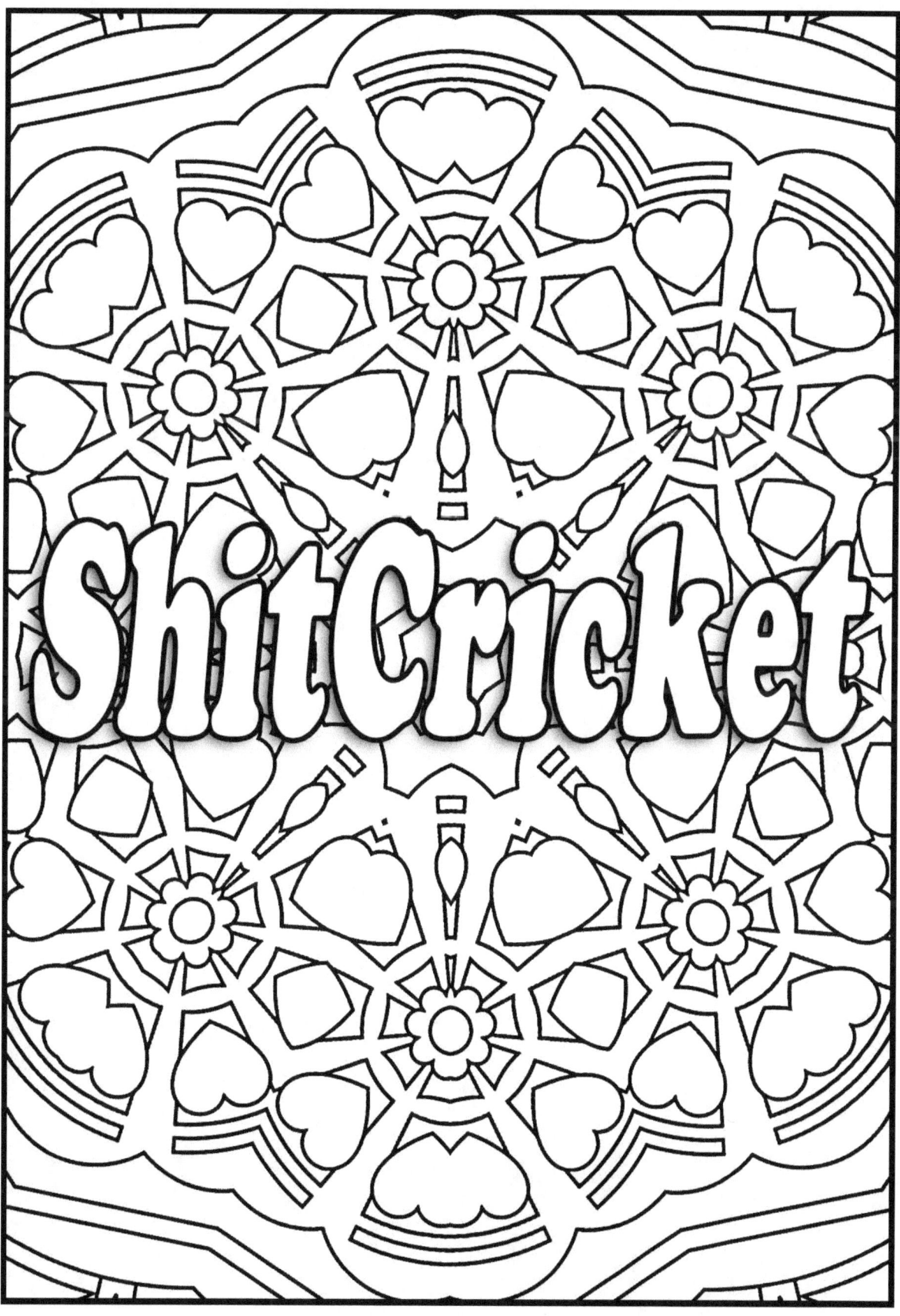

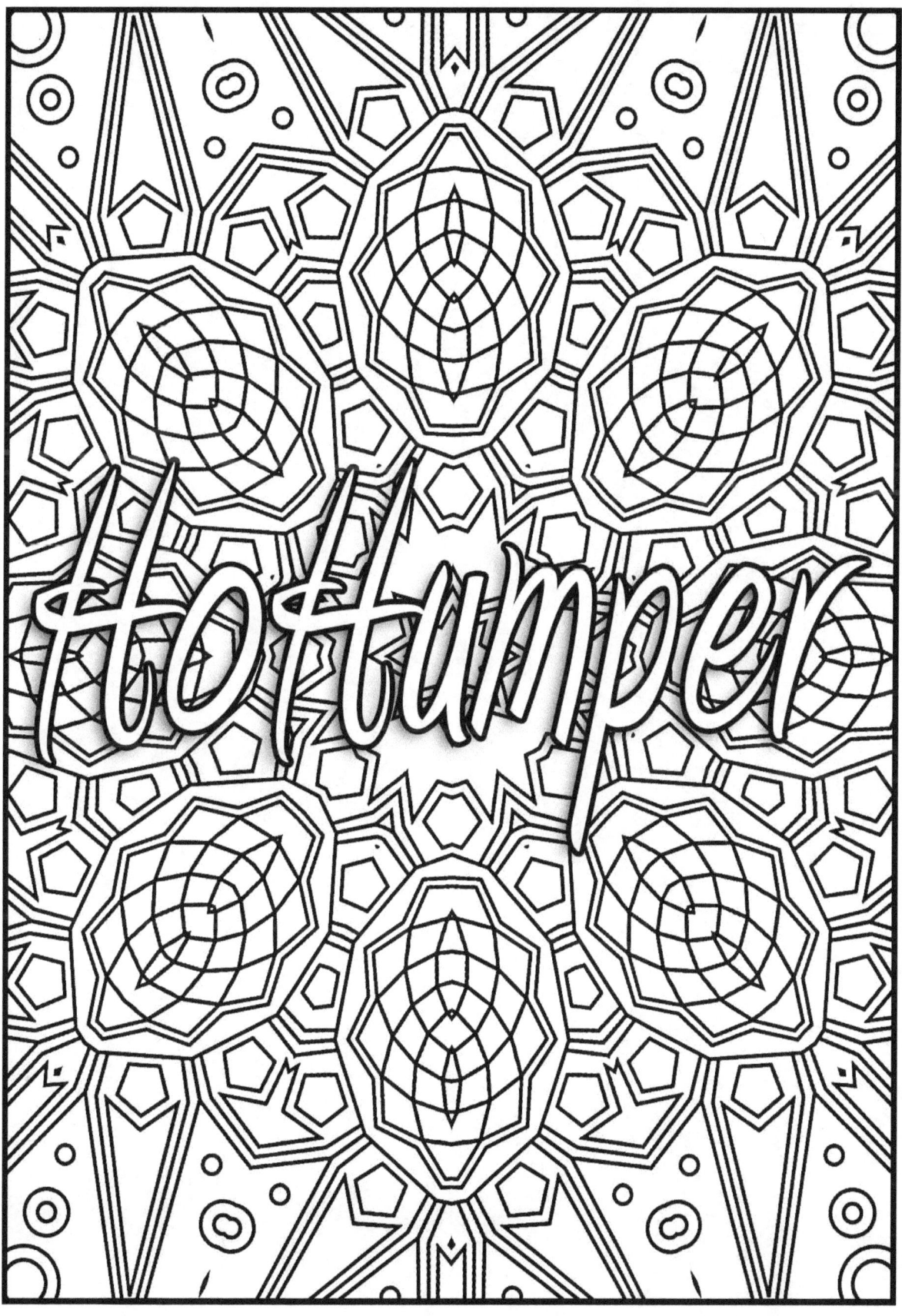

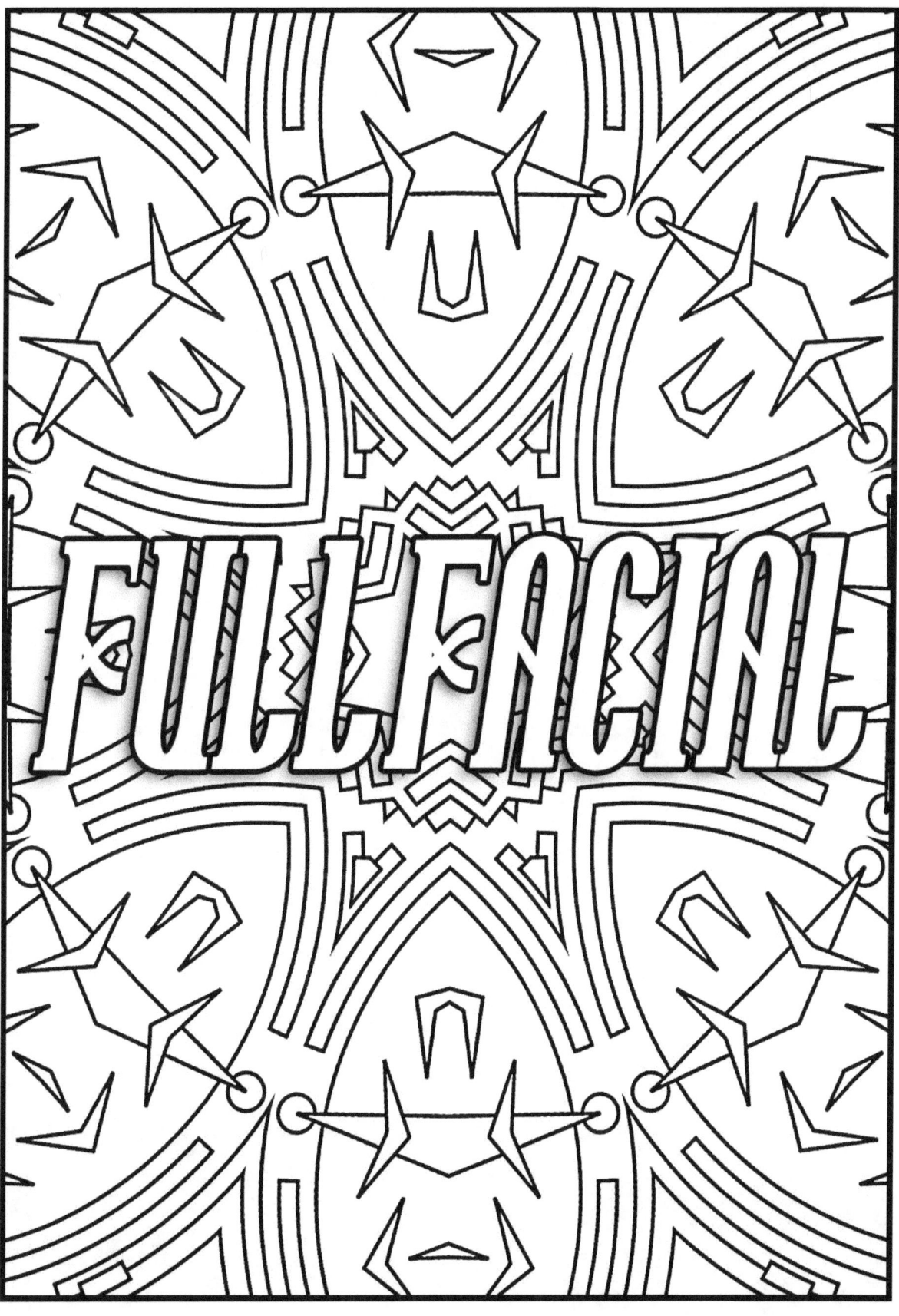

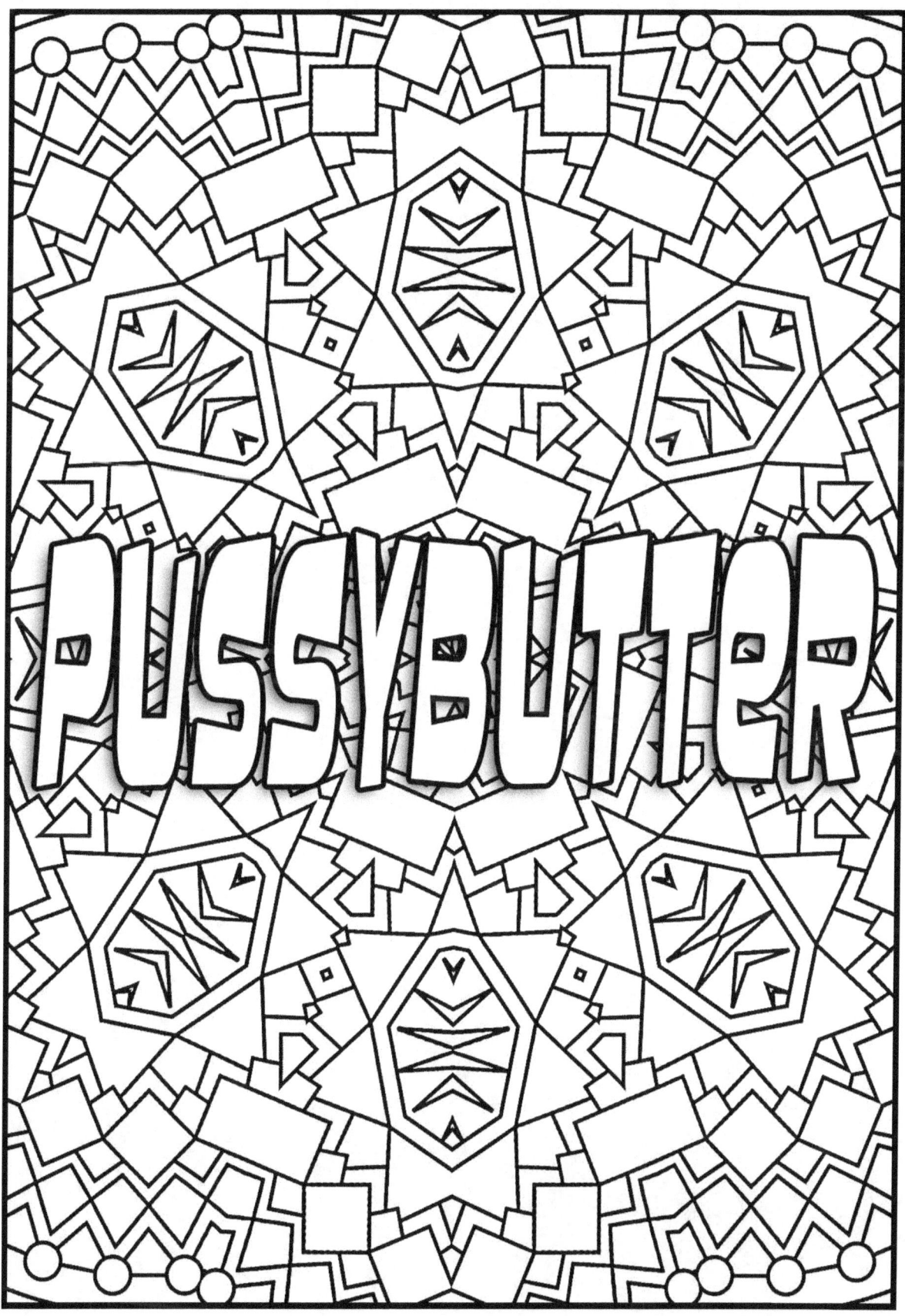

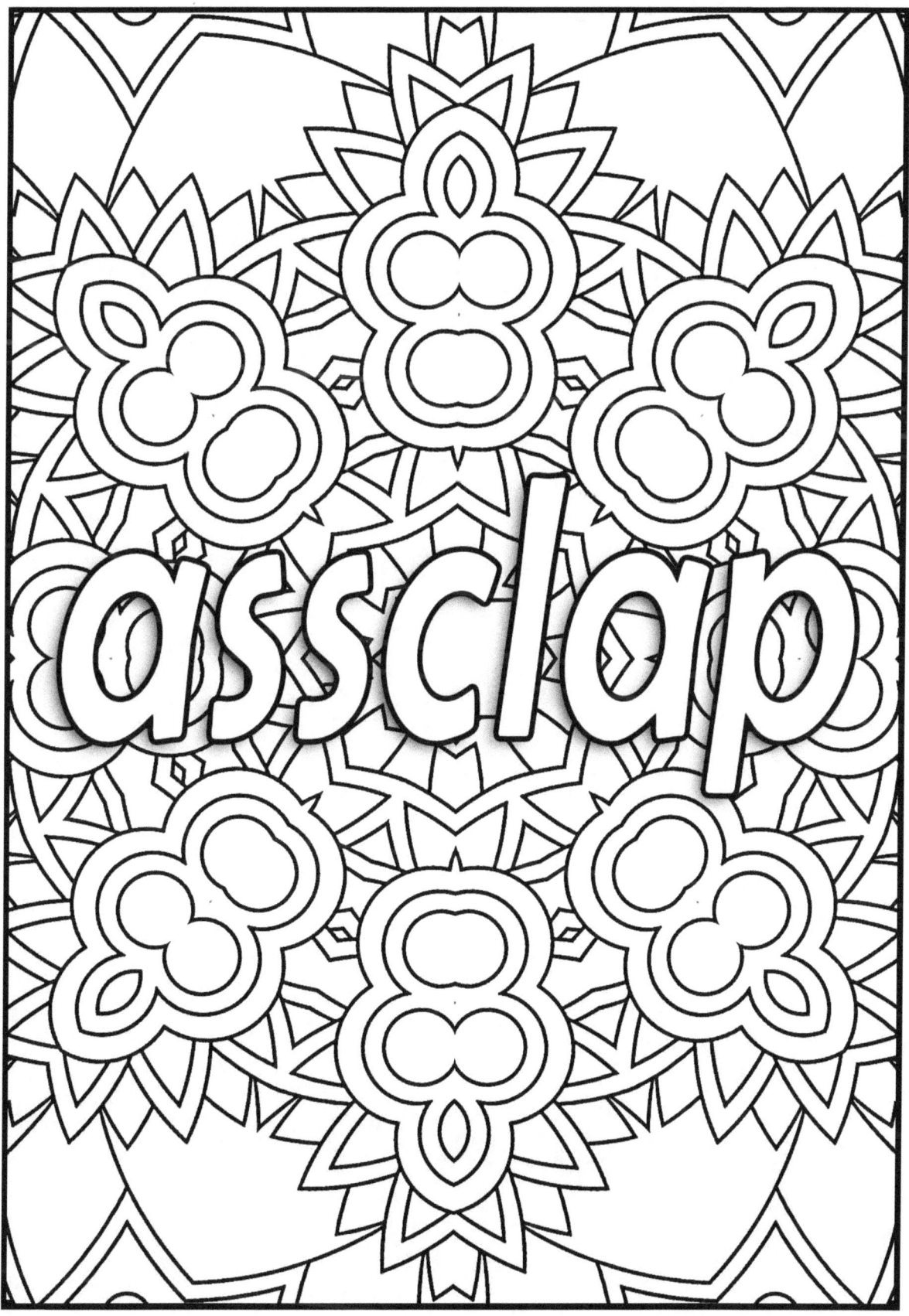

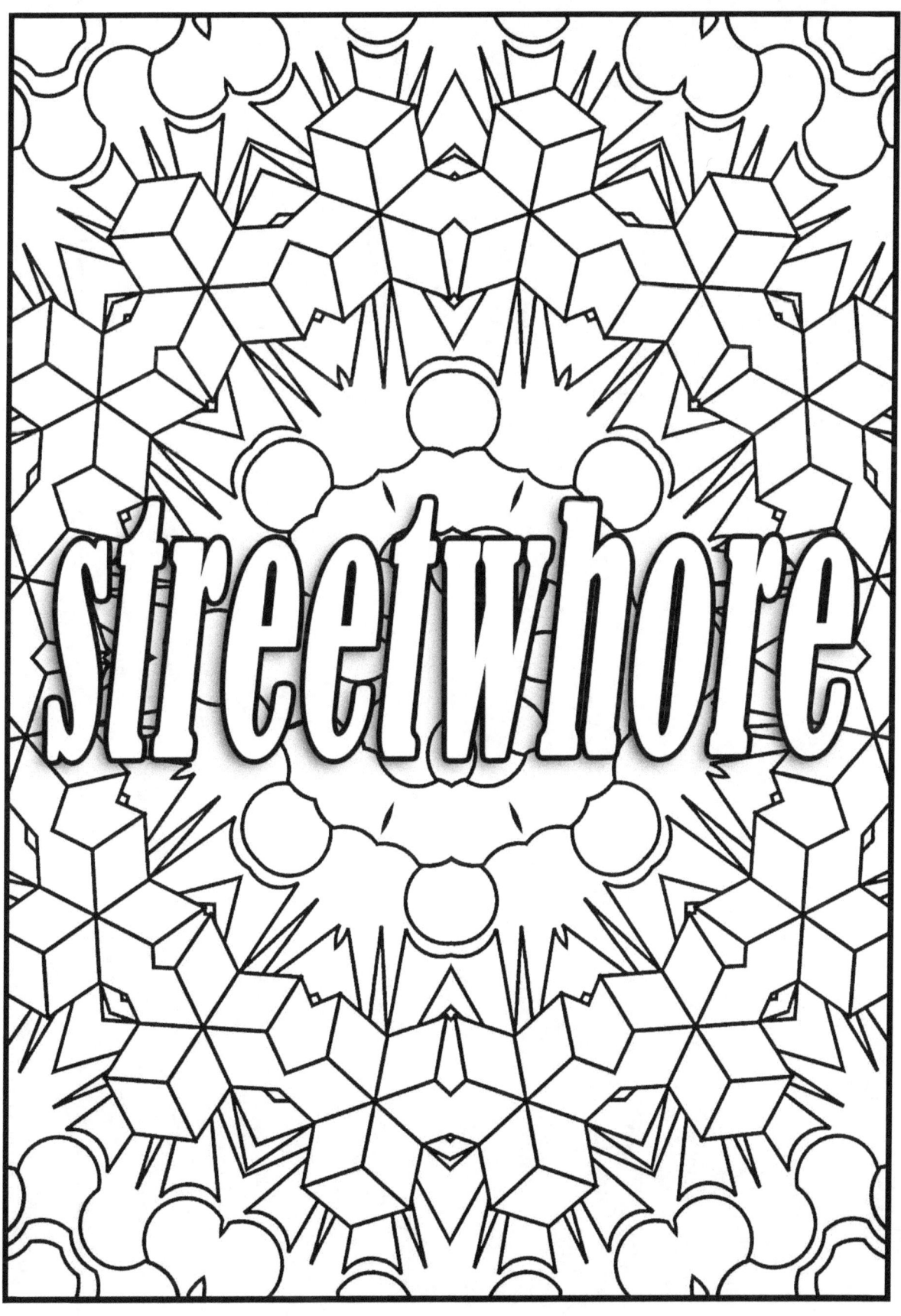

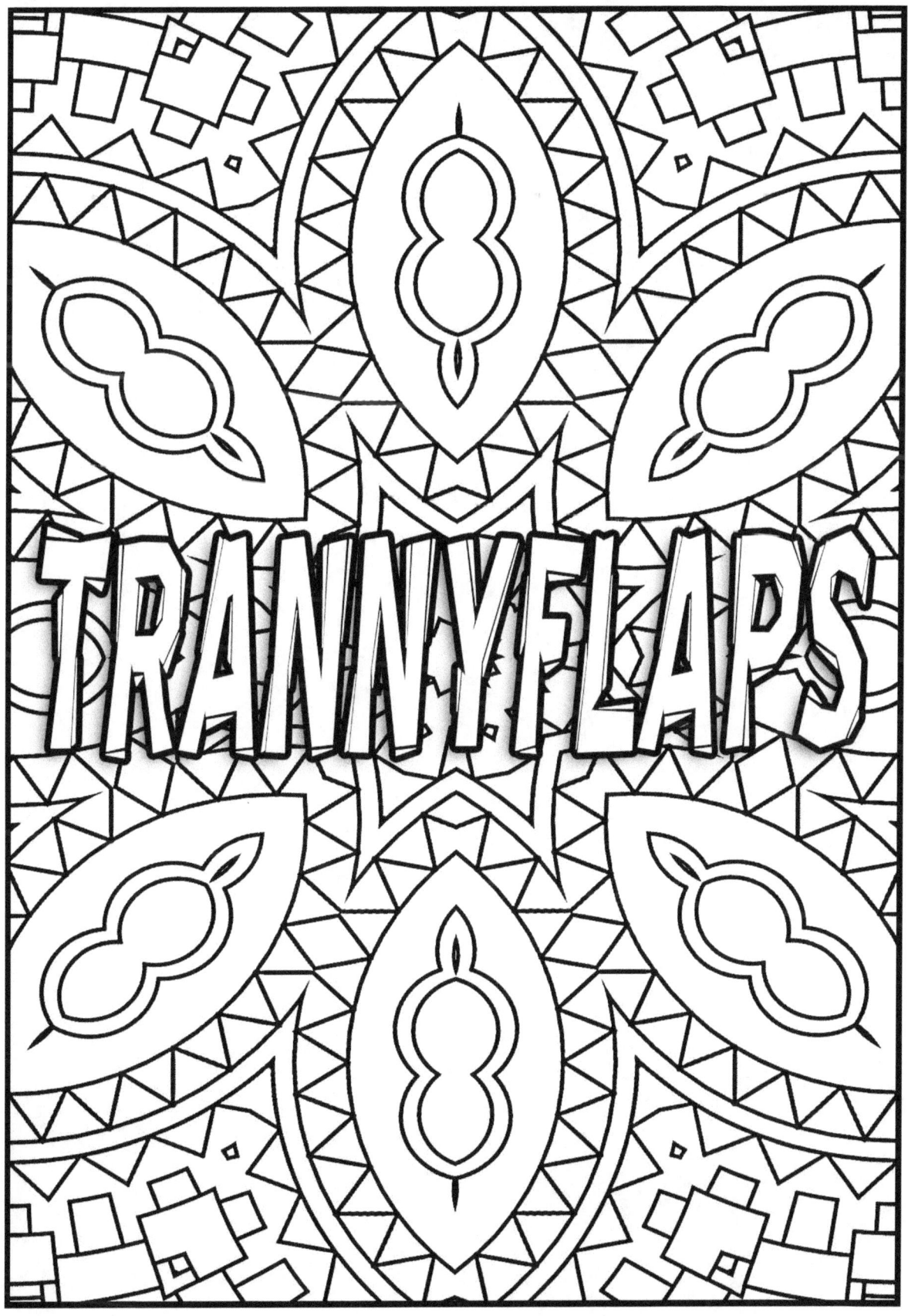

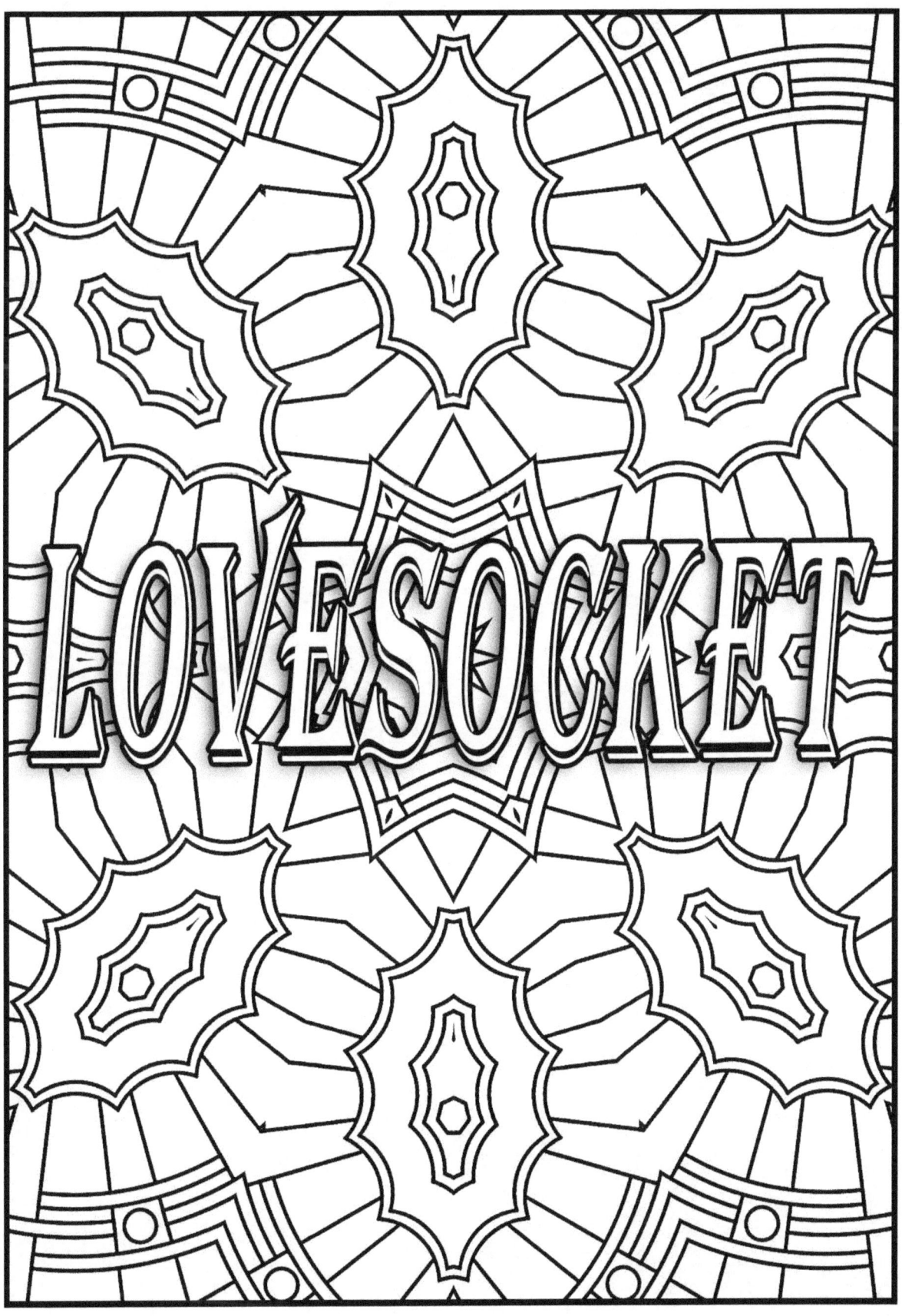

www.ingramcontent.com/pod-product-compliance
Lightning Source LLC
Chambersburg PA
CBHW080612190526
45169CB00007B/2985

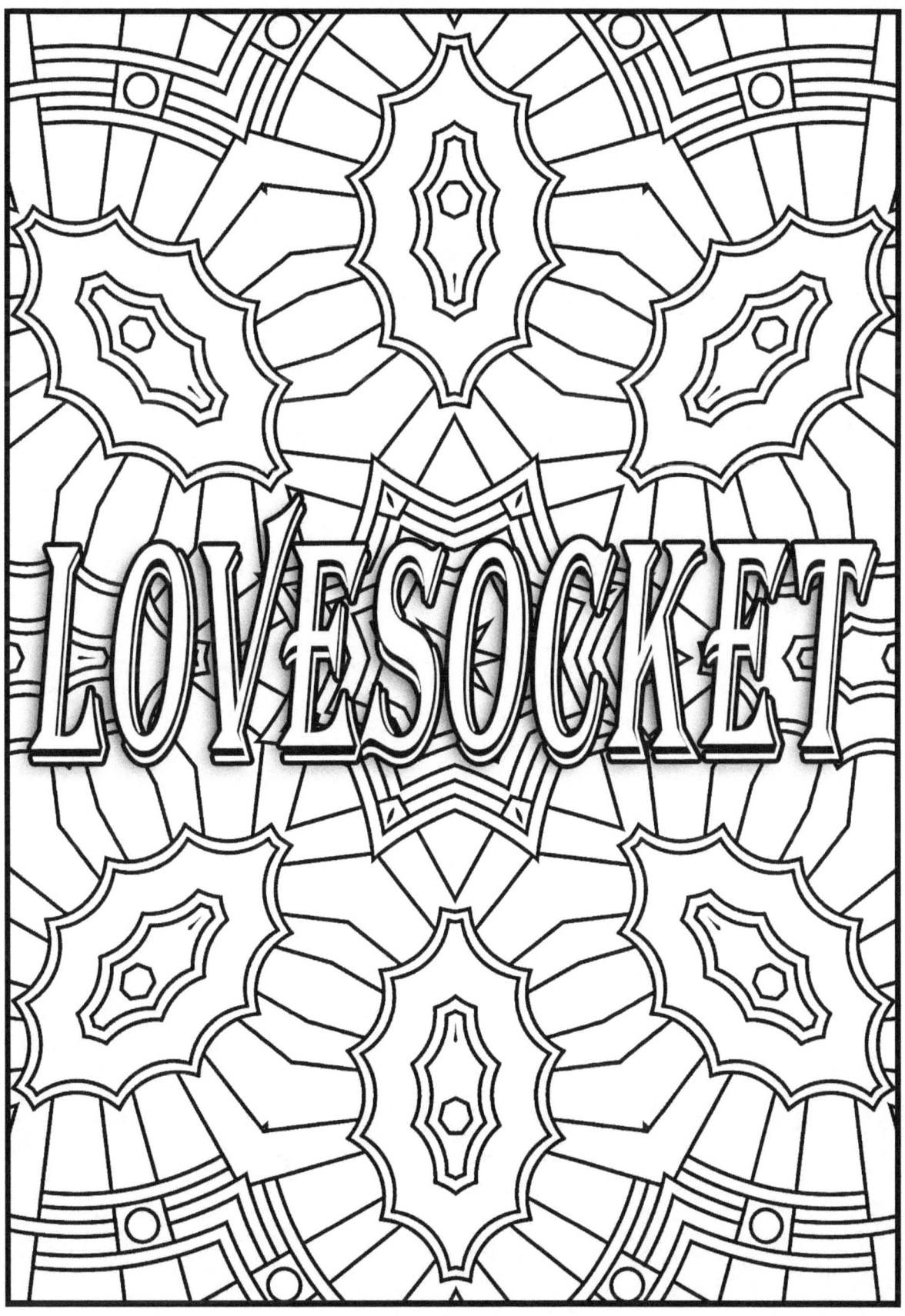

www.ingramcontent.com/pod-product-compliance
Lightning Source LLC
Chambersburg PA
CBHW080612190526
45169CB00007B/2985